MANJIRO

The Boy Who Risked His Life for Two Countries

EMILY ARNOLD McCULLY

Farrar Straus Giroux
New York

"No Japanese ship or boat . . . nor any
native of Japan, shall presume to go out of the
country; whoso acts contrary to this shall die."
—Tokugawa Shogunate pronouncement, 1638

In 1841 a boy named Manjiro lived with his widowed mother and sisters and brothers in a village called Nakanohama in the province of Tosa in Japan. His father had been a fisherman, so, according to custom, Manjiro would become one, too.

Even though he was barely fourteen years old, Manjiro persuaded a fisherman to hire him. There were five men on the little boat when it set off for fishing grounds a few miles from shore. For several days, they moved from one area to another, catching mackerel. But then ominous black clouds appeared, followed by ferocious winds, and suddenly the boat began to founder in the stormy sea. The fishermen tried to head for shore, but an oarlock broke off and the oar itself was washed overboard. The boat was borne southeast, at the mercy of freezing winds.

The men were afraid they would never find their way back home and that if they did, they would face the executioner. For over two and a half centuries Japan had been closed to the outside world. Anyone who tried to return after leaving the country could be put to death. But Manjiro told himself over and over again that somehow he would return to his mother.

After eight sea-tossed days, the terrified fishermen approached a rocky island near nightfall. They waited until morning before swimming for shore. Their boat was smashed to pieces against the rocks and one man's leg was badly injured.

No one lived on the tiny island, but the men discovered a cave and decided to make it their home. Manjiro found rainwater in a few stony crevices and everyone scooped it into their parched mouths. There were hundreds of nesting albatrosses on the island. Meat and eggs to keep them all alive!

But in the months that followed, little rain fell. The castaways each agreed to sip only three small shells of saved rainwater per day, and everyone kept his promise. Once, a ship appeared on the horizon. The men jumped up and down, shouting into the wind, but the vessel passed by. A few weeks later, the island rumbled and shook. An earthquake! That, too, they survived. In one of their searches of the island, they stumbled onto a pair of graves—those of castaways like themselves? The men wept, imagining that someday seafarers would find their own remains.

Manjiro kept watch on the horizon.

In the sixth month of the castaways' ordeal, a huge ship came into view. Two small boats were lowered and men began to fish. Manjiro shouted and two of his mates hurried to help signal to them. The men in the boats raised their hats in acknowledgment. Rescued! Manjiro thought, and hurled himself into the sea.

A dark giant lifted him out of the water. "There are others on the island," Manjiro told the men on the boat. They stared blankly. He gestured toward the rocks. Finally, they seemed to understand. His fellow fishermen were found and brought aboard.

The men spoke to them in a strange language. No one understood a word. The fishermen were taken to the huge ship where they met the captain, clearly a noble man, whose quarters were as beautiful as a shrine to Buddha. They were given food and ridiculous garments to put on. The captain showed them how to close the buttons and put on shoes made of animal hide. In Japan it was a crime to make clothing out of animal skins. Manjiro walked the length of the fantastic ship. How did it steer a course over the deep ocean, so far from any landmarks? he wondered.

The fishermen were led to hammocks belowdecks, but Manjiro was too curious to stay down there. The sailors paid no attention to him, so he followed them, trying to make sense of what they were doing. When they spoke, he repeated their words. Now they took notice. One said *mast* to him, pointing. Manjiro repeated the word. The others laughed and took turns teaching. *Rope. Deck. Compass. Sextant. Potato.* The ship itself was called the *John Howland.*

The next day, the captain gestured to Manjiro to get into a small boat and return to the island. Manjiro burst into tears. Was he being sent back? "No, no," the captain said. He simply wanted Manjiro to fetch the men's belongings from the cave.

The captain's name was William H. Whitfield, and he gave Manjiro a slate with letters on it. "The alphabet," he said, and helped Manjiro practice writing the letters. Manjiro quickly learned them by heart. He tried to teach his countrymen, but they had no interest in foreign ways. They did their share of work on the ship, however.

The Americans began calling him John Mung (short for Manjiro). He became Captain Whitfield's shadow. Could he stand watch in the crow's nest? The captain said he could. One day, Manjiro saw the telltale spout and gave the cry *"Thar she blows!"* which sent the *John Howland* in pursuit of a whale. Small boats were lowered, each holding six men, one with a harpoon. They chased the animal for hours, finally killing it. They chained it alongside the ship and cut the blubber into chunks to be boiled down. Manjiro was awed. In Japan whales were snared in nets cast from the shore.

Captain Whitfield showed him how to read a map and use a sextant. He even let his eager pupil take the helm and steer the ship. "You could become a navigator," he told Manjiro, adding, "You learn quickly because you are fearless."

The *John Howland* stopped at the port of Honolulu, on the Sandwich Islands, for supplies. The fishermen asked to be left there to find jobs. Captain Whitfield said to Manjiro, "I would like you to come with me to Massachusetts." Manjiro wanted very much to stay with Captain Whitfield. The captain asked the oldest fisherman, the one who had hired Manjiro, for permission to take him to America. After a few moments, he gave it. Manjiro bowed to his fellow survivors. They had endured terrible things together. But now he would follow his own course. He tried to tell Captain Whitfield how grateful he was.

The *John Howland* left Honolulu to catch more whales before heading home, around Cape Horn.

When they arrived in New Bedford, Massachusetts, a few months later, the harbor bristled with the masts of great ships. Manjiro marveled at the drawbridge linking New Bedford and Fairhaven, the whitewashed buildings, the lofty spires, and the well-dressed men and women strolling side by side. A few people stared at him with suspicion.

Captain Whitfield took Manjiro to church so they could give thanks for their safe return. The church deacon hurried over and whispered, "The boy can't sit here. He must go to the Negro section." The captain stood and led Manjiro out of the church. He found another one that allowed them to sit together.

Captain Whitfield's house in Fairhaven wasn't ready for occupancy, so he lodged Manjiro with a neighbor whose daughter was a schoolteacher. She began tutoring him in English and the other subjects he would need to know before he could go to the school in town. Manjiro worked hard on his penmanship.

Captain Whitfield got married and bought a farm. In Japan, farmers ranked far above fishermen. Manjiro learned how to plant, cultivate, and harvest crops. He rode a horse, something only a samurai could do at home. If only his brothers and sisters could see him now!

At school, without the protection of the tall captain, Manjiro braved the silent stares of students. He was older than the other children, but he knew much less. So he studied hard to catch up. The boys called him a "bookworm." A classmate named Job Tripp told them to stop teasing the foreign boy, but even he avoided walking with Manjiro after school.

Sometimes Manjiro climbed to the captain's attic, where his kimono, carefully washed and mended, was stored. At night, Manjiro worried about his mother, wondering if the family had enough food. Did his disappearance bring disgrace to them? He was homesick for the sound of the temple bell, the pagoda, the singing and dancing and sweet cakes of cherry blossom time. He remembered floating a lantern down the river to guide his father's soul. In America, the seasons came and went and people worked, but they didn't pause to celebrate nature's beauty.

Manjiro cut branches from a cherry tree and took them to school. He explained to the teacher that he was observing the cherry blossom festival celebrated in Japan.

When summer came, he caught crickets and put them in a cage he made of sticks. "What's that for?" Job Tripp asked. "It's a Japanese custom," Manjiro said. "We like to hear them sing." He showed Job how to fill lanterns with fireflies and told him about the samurai, who were not only warriors but teachers and artists as well.

By the end of the term, Manjiro ranked first in his class. He was delighted when Captain Whitfield suggested that he study navigation at Bartlett's Academy.

The captain left on a two-year whaling voyage and put Manjiro in charge of his wife and baby son. Having unwillingly forsaken his Japanese family, Manjiro took special care of his American one. In town, men now tipped their hats to him, and women smiled cordially. More and more, people wanted him to tell them about the country he had come from.

Meanwhile, Manjiro was hatching a plan: he would earn enough money to buy a small whaleboat and put it aboard a ship bound for the Pacific. Once within range of Japan, he would row to shore and try to persuade the authorities to take him back. He knew how to navigate now and could translate his knowledge from English to Japanese and back again. He had acquired many other skills and studied the machines and tools that would enable his country to join the modern world.

One day Manjiro ran into the harpooner from the *John Howland*. He had become the captain of his own ship, the *Franklin*, and offered Manjiro a job as steward. With Mrs. Whitfield's permission, Manjiro took it. Over the course of the long voyage, the captain suffered a breakdown and had to be put ashore in Manila. The crew voted for new officers. Manjiro had so impressed the other men they elected him boatsteerer. The post paid twice as much money, but it still wasn't enough to buy a vessel that would get him to Japan.

When Manjiro returned to Fairhaven in 1849, Captain Whitfield was home. Everyone was talking about the California gold rush and the fantastic fortunes men could make overnight. Manjiro decided the goldfields were his best chance to earn enough money for a boat. Manjiro and the Whitfields told each other it wasn't goodbye forever. Once again, Manjiro sailed around Cape Horn, this time to San Francisco.

Manjiro took a steamboat from San Francisco up the American River to Sacramento. He memorized the look of the amazing cauldron ship—another wonder to carry back to Japan! From Sacramento he hiked and rode horses to the goldfields in the Sierra Nevada.

Every day Manjiro looked for gold and every night he carefully sewed what he had found into his jacket lining and lay on it, sleeping fitfully. When he had saved enough, he rode into town before dawn, waited for the bank to open, and exchanged the gold for paper money. It had taken Manjiro just seventy days to collect gold dust worth six hundred dollars.

Manjiro returned to San Francisco and boarded a ship bound for the Sandwich Islands. When he arrived in Honolulu, he sought out his fellow castaways. He learned that one had died, one wished to remain in the islands, and two were eager to join him in attempting to return to Japan. Manjiro bought a small whaleboat and named it the *Adventurer*. American officials gave him a United States passport and an official letter declaring the country's friendly intentions. Manjiro packed his beloved navigator's handbook, a biography of George Washington, scissors, matches, a seagoing clock, various tools, and, as he had long planned, presents of sugar, coffee, and a looking glass for his mother.

The captain of the *Sarah Boyd* agreed to take the castaways and the *Adventurer* to the Ryukyu Islands off Japan's southern coast. Once there, the three men launched their little whaleboat and managed to guide it to shore.

The first people they met asked why they were wearing such odd clothing.
Manjiro explained that they were castaways come home. Government officials
soon appeared and marched the three to a village where they were shut up in a
farmhouse and questioned. Would they be put to death, as the old law decreed?

Manjiro begged the jailers to send word to his mother, but they refused.
Instead, officials hurled questions at the men for seven long months. Were the
Americans planning to invade? What had Manjiro done in America? Had he
engaged in business? Why were American ships so large? Was it true that they
moved by the magic of fire?

The prisoners were transferred by boat to the port of Nagasaki on another island and questioned again. Manjiro told of railroads, steamships, the telegraph, whalers, drawbridges, and wristwatches, which were worn even by American children. He drew pictures and showed them his navigator's handbook. America will not invade us, he insisted. It wants only to trade with us. An artist was summoned to transcribe and illustrate Manjiro's account. Finally, the men were allowed to return to their villages.

The closer Manjiro got to his village of Nakanohama, the faster his heart beat.
Was his mother even alive? He had been gone for nine years. People were waiting
along the road for a glimpse of him. They surrounded him as he entered the
village. The crowd parted, and there stood his mother. He bowed deeply and
she burst into tears of joy.

"I thought you were dead!" she cried. "We made a tombstone and floated
a lantern for your soul. Oh, pride of my heart, you are home at last!"

Manjiro knew that he had two homes now, one in Japan and another in
America.

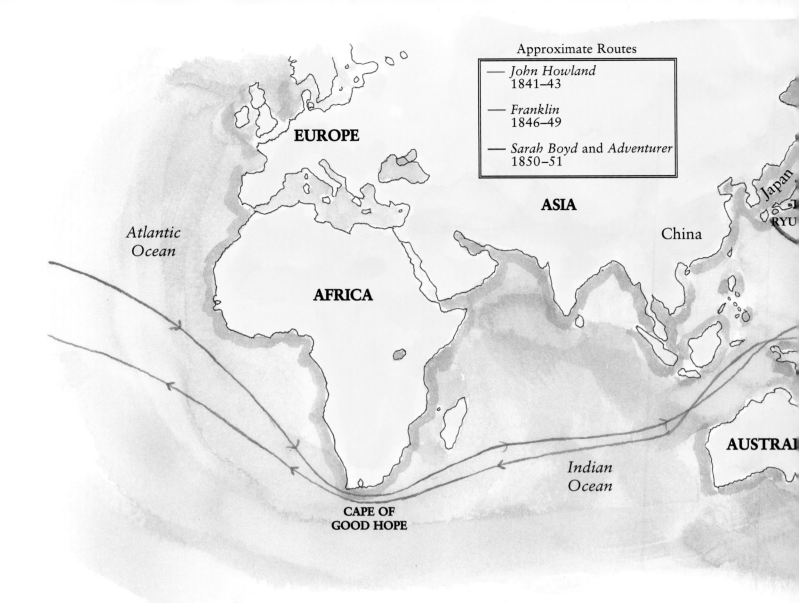

AUTHOR'S NOTE

The Tokugawa government of Japan (1603–1867) managed to close itself off from the rest of the world for over two hundred fifty years. With laws severely restricting personal freedom, the nation nevertheless prospered and produced magnificent works of art and literature. Guns and contact with foreigners were forbidden; a single Dutch trading ship that visited once a year provided the country's only contact with outsiders.

In the early American republic, Yankee traders doing business with China and New England whalers plying the Pacific sometimes picked up Japanese castaways and deposited them in the Sandwich Islands (now called Hawaii) or China. Manjiro and his shipmates were found on Torishima Island.

New Bedford, Massachusetts, and its neighbor, Fairhaven, were among the most diverse towns in the world. Whaling had brought seamen from all over the globe and produced immense wealth for the towns. The *John Howland*, with Manjiro aboard, returned a few months after Herman Melville departed on the famous whaling voyage that inspired *Moby-Dick*. And in this 1851 novel is the notable prophecy: "If that double-bolted land, Japan, is ever to become hospitable, it is the whale-ship alone to whom the credit will be due; for already she is on the threshold."

When Manjiro and his mates returned to Japan, their interrogation was recorded by the court. But the interrogators had trouble comprehending the things Manjiro described, so a scholar and illustrator

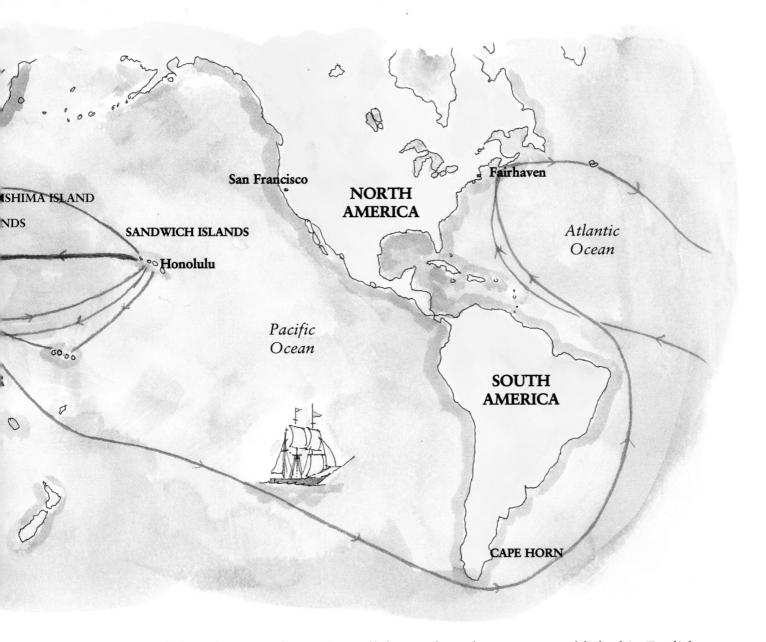

wrote and depicted the tale. He and Manjiro collaborated on the account, published in English as *Drifting Toward the Southeast.*

During the reunion with his mother, Manjiro was called away to the capital. The government was finally eager to hear everything he knew. Soon afterward, Admiral Matthew Perry and his "Black Fleet" of U.S. Navy ships arrived and demanded that Japan open its ports to American ships. Manjiro was asked to advise the Japanese leaders behind the scenes, and he helped assure his government that the United States wanted to trade, not to conquer. Because of Manjiro, the Americans noted with surprise, the Japanese already knew about such things as railroads and steamships. The two countries signed a peace treaty in 1854. Before long, Japan began to westernize, following many American models.

Manjiro was made a samurai, and he taught English, world history, and geography to other samurai. He returned to America as a member of the first diplomatic delegation sent to the West and was able to see his beloved Captain Whitfield once more. Manjiro died in 1898.

Ever since the end of the nineteenth century, Japanese admirers of Manjiro have come to Fairhaven and New Bedford to pay tribute to the towns that took in their young countryman and encouraged him to help forge a bond of friendship between the two nations.

BIBLIOGRAPHY

Benfey, Christopher. *The Great Wave: Gilded Age Misfits, Japanese Eccentrics, and the Opening of Old Japan.* New York: Random House, 2003.

Blumberg, Rhoda. *Shipwrecked!: The True Adventures of a Japanese Boy.* New York: HarperCollins, 2000.

Kaneko, Hisakazu. *Manjiro, the Man Who Discovered America.* Boston: Houghton Mifflin, 1956.

Manjiro, John, and Kawada Shoryo. *Drifting Toward the Southeast: The Story of Five Japanese Castaways.* Translated by Junya Nagakuni and Junji Kitadai. New Bedford, Mass.: Spinner Publications, Inc., 2003.

Plummer, Katherine. *The Shogun's Reluctant Ambassadors: Japanese Sea Drifters in the North Pacific.* Portland, Ore.: Oregon Historical Society Press, 1991.

Warinner, Emily V. *Voyager to Destiny: The Amazing Adventures of Manjiro, the Man Who Changed Worlds Twice.* Indianapolis: Bobbs-Merrill, 1956.

Other Sources

http://www.manjiro.org/manjiro.html

http://www.whalingmuseum.org/online_exhibits/manjiro/index.html

Thanks to Raiko Sassa at the Japan Society, New York City; Carolyn Longworth, librarian, and Debbie Charpentier, archivist, at the Millicent Library, Fairhaven, Massachusetts; and Jay Avila at Spinner Publications, New Bedford, Massachusetts

The photograph of Manjiro that appears in the author's note is from the Collection of the Millicent Library in Fairhaven, Massachusetts.

Library of Congress Cataloging-in-Publication Data
McCully, Emily Arnold.
    Manjiro : the boy who risked his life for two countries / Emily Arnold McCully.— 1st ed.
        p.   cm.
    Includes bibliographical references.
    ISBN-13: 978-0-374-34792-5
    ISBN-10: 0-374-34792-1
    1. Nakahama, Manjiro, 1827–1898—Juvenile literature.   2. Castaways—Japan—Biography—Juvenile literature.   3. Japan—Relations—United States—Juvenile literature.   4. United States—Relations—Japan—Juvenile literature.   I. Title.

DS881.5.N3M33 2008
952'.025092—dc22
[B]

2007026929